The Sayings of Chairman Malcolm

OTHER BOOKS BY MALCOLM S. FORBES

The Forbes Scrapbook of Thoughts on the Business of Life

Fact and Comment

The Sayings of Chairman Malcolm

THE CAPITALIST'S HANDBOOK

Malcolm S. Forbes

HARPER & ROW, PUBLISHERS
NEW YORK, HAGERSTOWN
SAN FRANCISCO, LONDON

Portions of this work originally appeared in *Forbes* magazine.

 For information address Harper & Row, Publishers, Inc., 10 East 53rd Street, New York, N.Y. 10022. Published simultaneously in Canada by Fitzhenry & Whiteside Limited, Toronto.

FIRST EDITION

Designed by Sidney Feinberg

ISBN 0-06-011359-6
LIBRARY OF CONGRESS CATALOG NUMBER: 77-11532

Dedicated to Ruth Gruenberg

and Bob Abboud; Alan Abelson; Patricia Aburdene; Rodney Acraman; Ray and Dorothy Adam; Jack Adams; Tom and Mary Adams; Maria Francesca Adelmann; Bachir Afia; Bill and Diane Agee; John Ahern; Roger Ahlbrandt; Bjorn Ahlstrom; Don Aidney; Ambassador A. Lel Alami; Annalita Alexander; Jimmy Alexander; Prince Alexander and Princess Barbara of Yugoslavia; Dewitt and Cynnie Alexandre; His Excellency Mr. Mowaffek Allaf; Brooke Allen; Fred and Charlotte Ann Allen; Douglass and Cynthia Alligood; Carl Ally; Susan Alsop; Frank and Frances Alspaugh; Pete Althoff; Norma Altman; Manny Alvarado; B. Charles Ames; Cleveland Amory; John Andersen; Betty Anderson; Bill and Janice Anderson; Bill and Josephine Anderson; Bob Anderson; Bob and Diane Anderson; Roger Anderson; Charles Andes; Premier and Mrs. Giulio Andreotti; Cliff Andrews; Ambassador Walter Annenberg; Alex Apsis; Alex Aranyos; Joti Are; Bill Armstrong; Eugene Armstrong; Bill Arnold; Louis and Joan Aronson; Jean Arre; Giles Artur; Roy Ash; Frank Ashburn; Chil and Candy Ashmun; Frank and Nancy Askin; Yousef Assed; Brooke Astor; Orin and Kathryn Atkins; C. Atonio; Louis Auchincloss; Paul and Jeane Austin; Fredo Ayala; Dana Backus; Elizabeth Bailey; Joe and Barbara Bailey; Don Bain; Agnes Baird; Cliff and Jane Baker; Bill and Sue Balderston; Bob Baldwin; Russ and Mary Ball; Mike and Nancy Ballantyne; Howard Ballew; Jim and Lynne Bama; Roger Baneman; Russell and Janice Banks; Abderrahim Baouabid; Chuck and Lois Barber; Bernard Barenholtz; Abdally Abdel Bari; Harry and Margaret Barker; Robby and Mary Barker; Cedge and Nini Barksdale; Carlyle Barnes; Leslie Barnes; Tracy Barnes; Wallace Barnes; Luis Barrenechea; Frank Barry; Ted Bartek; Robert Bartley; Charles Barton; Mary Bartow; Georges Basiliou; Ray and Joan Bateman; Michael and Jan Bates; Harlan Batrus; Mil Batten; Lionel Beakbane; Betty Beale; Steve Bechtel; Jane Becker; Jack and Marge Beckett; Tom Beebe; Bill Beekman; Bob and Mary Beekman; France Aimee Beekman; Steve and Dany Beekman; Herb and Joan Beggs; Leo Begleiter; Tevita Beka; Jackie Bell; Howard Ballew; Viktoria Belosevic; Sandy Bemis; Benami; Joan Bender; Hubert and Myriam Benedic; Kathy Benefiel; Ambassador Ali and Jacqueline Bengelloun; Audrey Bennett; Housni Benslimane; Bill Benton; David and Serena Beretta; Jane Berezin; Bernd Berg; Polly Bergen; Frank Berger; Bun Berkeley; Pearl Berkowitz; Phyllis Berman; Nell Bernhardt; Jean Bernkopf; Marcia Berss; Ben and Anne Biaggini; Ben and Polly Bidwell; Heinz Biel; Jack and Marion Bierwirth; Ken Bilby; Mickey and Harriet Biondo; Ambassador Abdullah Y. Bishara; Glenn and Pauline Bixby; Gary Blaettler; Simon and Olivia Bland; Sadie Blasi; Bob Bleiberg; Charlie Bluhdorn; Mike Blumenthal; Paul Blustein; Archie Boe; Bill Boeschenstein; Ann Boggs; Harry Bolwell; Betty Bond; John Bookout; Dan Boone; Gray Boone; Bill and Gigi Boothby; Fred and Lucia Borch; Frank and Susan Borman; Grace Boscia; Marge Boselly; Mohamad Boucetta; Abdeslam Boumedi; Zohra Boumedi; Paul Bowles; Bill Boyhan; Thornton Bradshaw; Jim and Joan Brady; Nick and Kitty Brady; John Brainardi; Fred and Joan Brengel; Mary Lou Breslin; Mr. and Mrs. Frank Briganti; Jean Briggs; Al Brittain; Edward Brockie; Edgar Bronfman; Harry Brooks; John Brooks; John W. Brooks; Ted and Sallie Brophy; Dick and Donna Brown; Don Brown; Kathy Brown; Lee and Alice Cary Brown; Manning Brown; Werner and Bucie Brown; Alan Bruce; Donald Bruce; Gordon Bruce; Lynn Bruhn; John and Ann Brundage; Harry Bruno; Jim and Betty Bruton; Gray and Joannie Bryan; Austin and Meg Buck; Mrs. Leonard Buck; Bob and Polly Buckley; Fred Bucy; Edgar Buehler; Charles Buek; Bob Buffaloe; Dennis Bunder; Joe Buonaventura; Bill and Gloria Burch; Paul and Betty Burdett; Jack Burditt; John Burgoyne; Carol Burke; Jim Burke; Ned and Nancy Burke; Shirley Burnett; Don Burnham; Frank Burns; Auggie Busch; Gussie Busch; Alice Bush; John Bush; Bill and Betsy Butcher; Bill Byrne; Jim Byrne; Fletch and Peg Byrom; Sox Calder; Jim and Joan Callahan; Justin and Tiffany Callahan; Liz Callan; Michael and Barbara Camp; David and Virginia Campbell; Matthew Campbell; Robert Campbell; Jose Campelo; George and Connie Carden; Walter Cardin; Ray Carey; Ed Carlson; Dorothy Carnegie; Governor Julian Carroll; Frank and Anne Cary; Cliff Case; Weldon and Bea Case; Martin and Josephine Caserio; Al and Ellie Casey; Anne Casey; Edith Casey; Jim and Ann Casey; Sam Casey; Sam and Dean Casey; Buzz Cash; Tom Castleberry; Teri Catalano; Berdena Caterina; Henry and Jessica Catto; M. Caucau; Edward Cave; Ray Cave; Dick Caward; President and Mrs. Nicolae Ceausescu; Ahmed Chabou; Mustafa Chabou; Lester Chace; Sue Chace; Steve and Arleen Chafitz; Khadija Chairi; Denise Chambers; LaVerne Chandler; Charlie and Jean Chapin III; Alvah Chapman; Paul Charlap; Christopher and Maie Lee Chen; Joe and Mary Chipparullo; Dave Christiansen; Jim Cianelli; Antonio and Linda Ciccone; John Ciuffo; Bob Cizik; Howard Clark; Tom and Peggy Clausen; Graham and Frances Claytor; Tina Claytor; Curt and Courtney Cleland; Kip and Carol Cleland; George Clissold; George and Elsie Clover; Ted and Denny Clucas; Bobbi Cochran; Brad and Betsy Cochran; Mike Codd; Wim and Rachael Coder; Bill and Rosemary Codus; Helen Cody; John and Cynthia Coffin; Sylvia Cohen; Kitione Coka; Franklin Cole; Bud Collet; Ira Collings; Harker and Emily Collins; Phyllis Collins; Harry and Ginney Combs; Bruce and Tucker Comstock; Geoffrey and Holly Connor; Jack and Mary Connor; Anne Conway; Jack Conway; Edna Cook; Jim Cook; Joan Cook; John and Bev Cook; Dick Cooley; Nonnie Cooney; Doug and Dawnia Cooper; Eleanor Copeland; Gloria Coppo; Brian and Vicki Corbell; Inia Corerega; Anne Costa; Hugh Covington; Jock and Betsy Cowperthwaite; Jimmie Craig; Peggy Crane; Stan and Joan Crane; Denny and Ailsa Crawford; Catherine Creelman; Jack and Norma Creelman; Mae Crimmins; Fred and Leta Crist; Liz Cronin; Lou Crossin; Edgar Crossman; Henry Crown; Karen Cuddy; Brian Cullman; Gary and Linda Cummings; John and Alice Cummings; Betsy Cunningham; John Cunningham; Peter Curran; Charlotte Curtis; John Curtis; Leland and Betty Curtis; Sid Cutter; Mrs. Charles Suydam Cutting; Warner and Rosemary Dailey; Arnold Daly; Mimi Daly; Vinny Daly; Rocco and Natalie Dameo; Nicky D'Amico; Pat D'Amico; Marilyn Dammerman; Mary Ann Danner; Michele Darr; Earl and Terry Dashiell; Richard and Sherry Dashiell; Eroni Daunibau; Peter Davidson; Faith Davies; Otto and Helene Dax; Doris Dealaman; Mark Dean; Gladys deBathe; Jean and Sharon de Beauregard; Boul de Breteuil; John and Trudie deButts; Ed deCastro; Pat Deckelnick; Jo DeCrescenzo; Jose De Juan; Peni Dekedeke; Bill and Sally DeLancey; Edmond de la Rochefoucauld; Arnould de Montalembert; Thierry de Montalembert; Alix de Rothschild; Andre and Ivana de Saint Sauveur; Lynn Deutchman; Arnaud de Villars; Christo and Marsha Dewey; Del and Betsy deWindt; Bob and Betty Dickey; Simon Dickinson; Suliano Diligolevu; Clarence Dillon; Doug and Phyllis Dillon; George and Joan Dillon; Ginnie Dillon; Mr. and Mrs. John Dillon; Sandy and Ginna Dillon; Sidney and Dorrie Dillon; Barbara Dimeo; Mike Dingman; Ed and Marie Dodd; Evan and Donna Dodson; Fred Dolder; Charles Dollfus; Carolyn Dombrowski; Toko Donato; Bishop Horace Donegan; Ed Donovan; Hedley Donovan; Al D'Orazio; Dan Dorfman;

Francois and Osmane d'Orglandes; Jack and Ellen Dornan; Christene Douglas; Frederick Douglas; Noel and Flo Douglas; Robert Douglas; Bill Drake; Bob and Bea Drevs; Ray and Ruth Dubrowin; T A and Edwina Duckworth; Ed and Jean Duffy; Angier and Robin Duke; Jack Duncan; Chauncey and Marie Dunn; Edgar and Sandy Dunn; Jim and Patti Dunn; Al Durner; Lorraine Dusky; Al and Mary Duval; Maggie Dwyer; Hal and Nancy Eastman; Joe and Sheila Eberhardt; J. J. Edwards; Chris Efford; Jamie Ehrenclou; John Ehrenclou; John and Elizabeth Ehrenclou; Bob S. Eisenhauer; Yassin El-Ayouty; George Elges; Lahcen El Hihi; Koresi Elia; Paul and Jane Elicker; Elizabeth Eller; Karl Eller; Duncan and Molly Ellesworth; Bob and Gine Ely; John and Fran Emery; Jane Engelhard; Johnnie English; Jan and Elsebeth Engzelius; Don Ercole; Errol Ernstrom; Rose Eskononts; Dudley and Lynnie Evans; Jim and Rosemary Evans; Tom and Betty Evans; Jack and Allie Ewing; Everett Fahy; John Fairchild; Barbara Fallon; Walter and Shirley Fallon; Dominique and Marina Falque; Asa and Norma Farr; Bob Farrell; Frank Farwell; Lawrence Faulstich; Paul and Bette Feiring; Clay Felker; Millicent Fenwick; Fergie Ferguson; John and Dee Fery; Temple Fielding; John and Marlene Filer; Obbie and Moiny Filley; Patrick and Marion Filley; Michael and Naomi Findlay; Julie Fink; Nancy Finn; Raymond Fisher; George Fitts; Bob Flaherty; Queenie Flake; Jim Flanigan; Lynn Fleary; Denny and Karin Fleck; David Fleischmann; Chuck Fleming; Helen Fleming; Jim Fleming; John Fleming; Joyce Fleming; O.D. Fleming; Bob and Elaine Flowerree; Woody Flowers; Jack Flynn; Milton Folds; Paul Foley; Bob Foman; Aldie Forbes; Bertie Forbes; Betts Forbes; Bob Forbes; Bruce Forbes; Buck and Claudia Forbes; Campbell and Dottie Forbes; Catherine Forbes; Charlotte Forbes; Dana Forbes; Dick Forbes; Duncan Forbes; Hamish Jacynthe Forbes; Jonathan Forbes; Kip and Astrid Forbes; Malcolm and Carol Forbes; Moira Forbes; Nigel and Rosemary Forbes; Roberta Forbes; Sabina Forbes; Sandy Forbes; Serena Forbes; Steve and Bina Forbes; Tim Forbes; Wally Forbes; Henry Ford; Jerry and Betty Ford; Tom Ford; Mr. and Mrs. Bill Foreman; David Forgione; Ronald Fountain; Andy and Elaine Fowler; Eric and Frannie Fowler; Fred Fox; Lew and Marjorie Foy; Allan Frank; Zollie and Elaine Frank; Betty Franklin; Diane Freeman; Dick and Norma Freeman; Gaylord Freeman; George Frelinghuysen; Harry and Marian Frelinghuysen; Joe and Emily Frelinghuysen; Peter and Bea Frelinghuysen; Seth French; Don Frey; Seymour Fried; Eleanor

Friede; Mitchell and Lita Fromstein; Henry Frost; Nikki Frost; Gertrude Fuhr; Don Fulton; Bill Gaccon; John Gallager; Ed Gallagher; Tex Gallegos; Nick Galluccio; Gamal Gamaleddin; Mrs. Richard Gambrill; Ali Gammal; Ratu Sir and Mrs. Penaia Ganilau; Pat Gantz; Martin Garbus; Dan Garcia; Stretch Gardner; M. and Mme. Henri Garnier; Mrs. George Garrett; Don and Milly Garson; Cliff Garvin; Woodie and Lena Garvin; Lynn Gaspar; Viliame Gauna; The Honorable Gerard Gaussen; Ngurah Gedhe; Dick Gelb; Hal and June Geneen; Krome George; Tony Gerharz; Robert and Isabelle Gerofi; Ned Gerrity; John and Lois Gerstenmaier; Abdul Ghani; Abdelkader Gharbi; John Gibb; Vernon and Diana Gibberd; Ed and Josephine Giblin; Paul Gibson; Mark Gilbey; Brendan Gill; Edward and Marie-Helene Gilly; Tedi Gilmartin; Bob and Mary Gima; Chester Gittleman; Bob Glasser; H. R. H. The Duke of Gloucester; Catherine Goetz; Pete Goff; Bernie Goldberg; Lou Goldberg; William Goldberg; Paul Goldberger; Joyce Golden; Len Goldenson; Harrison Goldin; Hilda Golle; Bill and Dot Goodall; Lorraine Goodlein; Jerry Goodman; Rita Gordon; Jerry and Shirley Gore; Mohammed Maiz Gorfti; Tatsuro Goto; Rod and Lydia Gott; Lyt and Sis Gould; Bill and Sassy Grace; Peter Grace; Bob and Marjo Graff; Kay Graham; Eugene Gramm; Carol Grant; Mrs. Sidney Bradford Grant; Butch Granville; Della Grattan; Boyden Gray; Gordon and Nancy Gray; Luke Gray; Marie Gray; Clive and Jennifer Greaves; Ash Green; Len Greenberg; Maurice Greenberg; Gael Greene; Richard Greene; Ed Griffiths; Jeff Grigsby; Tom and Terri Grojean; Jimmy and Kate Gubelmann; Tom and Ann Guendel; Dolores Guilhot; Loel Guinness; John and Kay Gurash; Elmer Gustafson; Walter Guzzardi; Robert Haack; Karl Hafner; Gene Hagin; Warren Hall; Armand Hammer; Jake Hammer; Harry Hammond; Jack and Mary Jane Hanley; Arthur Hanrahan; Sally Hardesty; Henry Harnischfeger; John and Samma Harper; Everette Harris; Lou Harris; Billy Harris; Anne Harrison; Russell and Nancy Harrison; Ted and Doris Hartgrave; Fred Hartley; Joseph Hartman; Ray and Betty Hartz; Robert and Nancy Harvey; Margaret Harwood; William Haselton; His Majesty King Hassan II; Bob Hatfield; Gabe Hauge; Vera Hayden; Willie Hayden; Jim and Polly Hayes; Roger Haynes; Elenora Hedden; Frank Hedrick; John and Inge Heilmann; Bob Heimann; Ben Heineman; John Heinemann; Tom and Julie Heinsheimer; Drew and Jack Heinz; George and Nancy Helmer; Lynn and Lorraine Helms; Eileen Henderson; Bob and Dickie Hendrie; Croft Henry; Paul and Betty

Henson; Fred and Carol Herbel; David Herbert; Toby Herman; Richard and Johanne Herold; Anson and Ruth Herrick; Bob Herring; Ray and Jane Herzog; Bill Hewitt; William Hewlitt; Dick and Polly Hill; Barron Hilton; Bill and Jane Hobbs; Bruce Hoffer; Jerry Hoffman; Wayne and Laura Hoffman; Roy Holdt; Mr. and Mrs. Carl Hollis; Walter and Jean Holmes; Soichiro Honda; Basil and Rilda Hone; Lucien and Bernadine Hooper; John and Ellen Ann Hopkins; Mr. and Mrs. Charles Hopper; Dr. John Hornaday; Ed and Elizabeth Horrigan; Fred and Blan Hostetter; Jim and Karen Hotchkiss; Win and Jane Hotchkiss; Walter Hoving; Laiachi Howari; Ray Howe; Roger Howell; Susan Hubbard; Carter Hudlow; Jamie Hudlow; Jim and Woody Hudlow; Shaun Hudlow; Roger Hull; Hugh Hunt; Eleanore Hunter; Hank and Diane Hunter; Larry and Olivia Huntington; His Majesty King Hussein I; Bob and Char Hutton; William Hutton; Hugh and Cocky Musgrave Hyde; Mary Hyde; Lee and Mary Iacocca; Phyllis Iannelli; Wataru Ikeda; Qio Ilaitia; Estelle Insler; Jennie Irizarry; Bill and Susan Isbell; John Jay Iselin; Peter and Bonnie Iselin; Marsha Izak; Dahl Jack; Edna Jackson; Howie Jackson; Tom Jaffe; Walter Jaffe; General Jaidi; Bud James; Jim Jaquez; Rosemary Jarvie; Alec Jenkinson; Oliver Jensen; Yale Joel; Coddy and Ellie Johnson; Frank and Helena Johnson; Frank and Jo Johnson; Canon James and Leslie Johnson; Jimmy and Gretchen Johnson; Peter and Anne Johnson; Terry Johnson; Clarita Jones; Ernie Jones; Reg and Grace Jones; Thomas Lee Jones; Tom V. Jones; Jock Jordan; Elliot Kahn; John Kalpin; Sam Karen; Dino Kartelias; Howard Kates; Dick and Gay Kattel; Gloria Katz; Howard Kauffmann; Walter and Lillian Kavanaugh; Toroni Kawa; Dick Kazokas; John and Joan Kean; Tom Kean; Steve and Mary Keating; President Urho Kekkonen; Rodger and Joyce Kell; Gene Kelley; Ed Kelly; Kermit Kelly; Margee Kelly; Gordon Kemp; Jim Kemper; Ed Kennard; Jim Kerr; Jim Ketelsen; George Kidder; Peter Kiers; Michael and Mary Killeen; Les and Mary Kilpatrick; Bob Kimmerle; Kerryn and Shirley King; Max King; Doug Kinzel; George Kinzel; Francis "Doc" Kirby; Fred and Walker Kirby; Marylou Kirby; Bob and Barbara Kirby; John and Dottie Kircher; Boris and Barbara Kirilloff; John Kirkuff; Ashie and Sylvia Kissel; Peter and Phyllis Kissel; Coka Kitione; Viliame Kitu; Jonas Kjellberg; Dick and Arline Kline; Patton and Jean Kline; David and Patricia Klipstein; George and Rita Kneeland; Win Knowlton; Bunkie and Florence Knudsen; John and Dora Koch; Virginia Koehler; Hazel Koenig; Joseva

Kolinibaravi; Paul Kolton; Kolinio Komainalovo; Rudy Kopf; Emori Koroi; Bob Koshinsky; Bill Koslo; Michael Kramer; Louise Krepela; Oscar and Lisa Kruesi; Ray and Bobbie Kurshan; S. Kuruka; Delano and Sis Ladd; Ed and Shirley Laffey; Wynn Laffey; Peter Lagemann; Carter and Ruth Laidlaw; Henry and Mary Laidlaw; M. Lair; Abbie Laker; Roland and Florence Lamb; Matney Lambe; Din Land; Ellis Landau; Ward and Judith Landrigan; Lorrie Langford; Wally La Prade; Dr. and Mrs. Ahmed Laraki; Abdeslam Larossi; Dolores Lataniotis; Maria Latorraca; May Laube; Frank Lautenberg; Hal Lavine; Susan LaViola; Bill Lawrence; Harding and Mary Lawrence; Chris Lawther; David Leavitt; Julien and Priscilla LeBourgeois; Eppie Lederer; Tiko Ledua; Charlie and Sally Lee; Charlie Lee III; David Lee; Diana Lee; Lucy Lee; Micaela Lee; Rupert Legge; Lynn Leigh; Ted and Julie Leisenring; Pierre Lemaire; David Lerbs; Marvel Lesher; Gary Leslie; John Leslie; Tarka and Jane Leslie-King; Neil Letson; Jone Lewenilovo; Bill and Carole Lewis; Floyd and Jimmie Lewis; George and Phyllis Lewis; George and Ellen Lewis; Paul and Ibby Lewis; Paul and Phyllis Lewis; Ann Lewis-Smith; Princess Karoline of Liechtenstein; May Liedquist; Luisa Likuiviu; Jim Lilly; Flora Ling; Jim Link; Bill and Eleanor Lippincott; John Lobb; Vinnie Loccisano; Alison Locke; Marshall Loeb; John and Edna Logan; Josh and Nedda Logan; Viliame Loganimoce; David and Charlotte Look; Lucy Look; Screvie and Appie Lorillard; Lee Louie; Winslow and Jo Lovejoy; Bill Loverd; Jay Lowe; Jimmy Lowe; Mr. and Mrs. Robert Lowe; Hank Luce; David Luke; Robert Lund; Bob and Liane Lunny; John Lux; Paul and Dorothy Lyet; Earle MacAusland; Don Macdonald; Ray and Florence Macdonald; Gene Mack; Irene Mack; Russ Mack; Helen Mackay; Bud and Grey Mackay; Don and Winnie MacNaughton; Robert MacNeil; Philip Macomber; Ian MacPherson; Dick and Joan Madden; Nick Madormo; David Maestas; Frank Maestas; Lillian Maestas; Paul Maestas; Tom Maggio; David Mahoney; Alex Mair; Jona Maiwaikava; S. Malakai; Jim Mallon; Noa Malo; Robert and Ibby Malott; Christine Malski; Shirley Maltz; Herb and Gloria Maneloveg; Mike Mansfield; The Rt. Hon. Ratu Sir Kamisese and Adi Lady Lala Mara; Bill Marchman; Inez Marella; John Margaronis; L'Abbe Bernard Marie; John Marion; Jim and Ann Maritz; Bob Markiewicz; Herb and Nancy Markley; Steve Markman; Andree Markoe; Frank Markoe; Bill and Donna Marriott; Bill Marsteller; Annmarie Martorano; Gus Marusi; Gene and Mary Mason; Raymond Mason; Mike Masterpool; Alipate

Mataitoga; Dick Mau; George Mauro; Jack McAdams; Jerry McAfee; David McAlpin; Marguerite McBey; Trish McCaldin; Archie McCardell; Peter and Ginny McColough; Bob and Claire McConaughy; Brooks McCormick; Joyce McCracken; Mac McDaniel; Jane McDermott; Jim and Betty McDonald; Murray and Peggy McDonnell; Puddin McDonnell; James McDonnell; Sandy and Pris McDonnell; Russ McFall; John and Conna McGillicuddy; Brian McGlynn; Carl McGraw; Harold McGraw; Pat McGraw; Larry and Mary McKearney; John and Cleo McKinney; Earle McLaughlin; Ed McMahon; Bob McMearty; Barry McMennamin; Breeze McMennamin; Dunc McMillan; Bill McMurren; Jessie McNab; Joe McPhillips; Eugenie Mead; Dodds Meddock; Joe Medina; Sam Medina; Ambassador Adly Abdel Meguid; Leo and Betty Melamed; Drew and Fifi Mellick; Mrs. Roger Mellick; Jerry Melsha; Ellen Melton; Alan Meltzer; Arline Meltzer; Lou and Jane Menk; Binger and Traudell Menne; Al and Kate Merck; George and Betty Merck; Herman and Susan Merinoff; Harry Merlo; Hillie Merrill; Rodney and Genevieve Merrington; Bill and Monnie Messinger; John and Eleo Mettler; Ruben Mettler; Jim and Fran Michaels; Ted and Fritze Michaelsen; Carmen Micich; Joan Miles; Jacques and Monique Milet; Maryline Milet; Fred Milholland; Rose Millar; Bill and Ariadna Miller; E. L. Miller; Harriett Miller; Paul and Adele Miller; Paul and Cass Miller; Paul and Louise Miller; Gerrish and Phoebe Milliken; Minot and Edith Milliken; Roger and Nita Milliken; Weston Milliken; Michael Mims; Laury Minard; Arthur Mitchell; Robin Mitchell; Bill Moffett; Russ and Margaret Moir; Bill Monahan; Peter Monahan; Jack and Nancy Moody; Ed and Patty Moran; Ed Morgan; Sarah Morhaim; Hideaki Moriya; Barc and Annette Morley; Tom Morris; Bud and Peggy Morrow; May Morse; Teodor Moscoso; George and Mildred Moseley; J. B. and Fran Mosley; "Red" Motley; John and Marjorie Mullens; Ray and Sis Mulligan; David Mumma; Harvey and Melinda Mumma; Kenny Mumma; Nancy Mumma; Rupert Murdoch; Lewis and Bunny Murdock; Barry and Bev Murphy; Bob and Marge Murphy; Charles and Doris Murphy; Mike Murphy; Ray and Helen Murray; Martin Myers; Tupou Nakete; Mickey Nalewako; Richard Nalle; William Naumann; Tony Navarro; Henry Nawrocki; Otto and Margaret Nelson; Al and Lori Neuharth; Warren Nevins; Tim Newcomb; Clyde and Maggie Newhouse; Ed Newman; Steve and Marilyn Nicoll; Cook Nielson; Robbie Nierengarden; Niumaia Niumataiwalu; Vernon Noble; Governor Philip Noel; Robbie and

Mirelle Noirclerc; Bob and Trish Nolan; John Nolan; Harold and Betty Noling; Karlfried and Tina Nordmann; William Norris; Isaac and Josephine Northup; George Norton; Jim Norton; Julian Nott; Dan Nugent; Donald Nyrop; Jack O'Brien; Ralph and Barbara O'Brien; Frank O'Connell; Tom Oerman; Jim O'Gara; Jim O'Hanlon; Mark Oinonam; Dick and Lisa Oldenburg; Marian Oliva; Ann Oliver; Ken Olsen; Frank Olson; Larry Olson; Jerry O'Neil; Mike O'Neill; Steve Opiela; Harry Oppenheimer; Dorothy O'Reilly; Bob and Margaret Ormsby; John Ortega; His Excellency Ambassador Ahmed Osman; Ismail Osman; Warren and Wanda Pace; Ruben and Anna Pacheco; Rudy Pacheco; Donald Packer; Dot Padgett; Bill Paley; Dick Palmer; Josua Panapasa; Betty Papsdorf; Sal Parisi; Joe Parkhurst; Bill and Sally Pascoe; Pato; Andrew Patrick; Pat and Dorothy Pattberg; Pat and Anne Patterson; Ken Patton; Patsy Paul; Roger Paul; Ginny Payson; Dorothy Pazos; Luvie Pearson; Bob Peckham; Chuck Peebler; Lush Pell; Darrell Penning; Jon Perel; Stuart and Valerie Perkins; Mrs. Lester Perrin; Dora Perry; Edie Pershouse; Pat Persico; Barbara Peters; Pete Peterson; Frank and Laura Petito; Arthur Petz; Bob and Mary Pew; Anke Pflugbeil; Alex and Edith Pfotenhauer; Dick Phalon; Betty Phelan; Dick and Ruth Phelps; Bert and Helen Phillips; Marilyn Phillips; Mort and Abby Phillips; Tom Phillips; Warren Phillips; John and Nancy Pierrepont; Peggy Pierrepont; Bob Pierson; Chuck and Betty Pilliod; Dick Pinkham; Duncan and Kathy Pitney; Earle and Alice Pitt; Don and Peggy Platten; Bob Pliskin; Charles and Jean Plunket; Fred Pollock; Jean Pierre and Caroline Pommereau; Terry and Barbara Pope; Don Popp; Fred and Ronnie Port; Sylvia Porter; Ad and Sadie Posnick; Bill Potter; Rick Potts; Dick and Edi Powell; Jody Powell; Bob and Marian Powers; Dick and Pat Powers; Don and Catherine Powers; Odey and Elizabeth Powers; Susan Pritchard; Jay Pritzker; Arnie Prives; Jerry and Betty Probst; Arthur Pulsinelli; Sam Pupello; Dick and Maggie Purnell; Mrs. David McAlpin Pylé; John and Nancy Pyne; Mrs. H. Rivington Pyne; Percy and Evie Pyne; Rivy and Funny Pyne; Saula Qilitia; Ed Quenault; The Honorable C. Abdul Rachman-Ramly; Donna Radoman; Timou Raduadua; Apete Rakesa; Si Ramo; Christian Ramos; Joe Ramos; The Honourable Sir Peter and Lady Ramsbotham; Solomone Raqila; Lydia Raurell; Miguel Raurell; Josi Ravaga; Kalini Sei Rawaisavu; Semi Rawaisavu; Steve Read; Pete and Alice Redfield; Joel Redler; Bill and Min Rees; Dick and Martha Reeves; Don Regan; Jack and Prue Regan; Stan Regan;

Tom Reghanti; Henry Reichhold; Sharon Reier; Shlomo Reifman; Ken and Diana Rendell; Harry Repak; Bob Reuss; Pam Revere; Dave and Margy Reynolds; Dick Reynolds; John Rhein; Simon and Beata Reynolds; John and Thelma Riccardo; Stanley and Leona Rice; Tom Rice; George and Patsy Richards; Gil and Mitzi Richards; Reuben and Lisa Richards; Thomas Richmond; John and Jane Ricker; Eric and Tory Ridder; Bob Rideout; Richard Riley; Eric Rill; Rosemary Rintz; Rosemary Rizzo; Norman and Dutzie Robbie; Earl and Ruth Roberson; Mel Roberts; Jim Robinson; Sam and Carol Robinson; Walter and Margaret Ann Robinson; David and Peggy Rockefeller; Larry Rockefeller; Laurance Rockefeller; Nelson and Happy Rockefeller; Al and Connie Rockwell; Angel Rodriguez; Carlos Rodriguez; Henry Rodriguez; Joe and Mercy Rodriguez; Virgil Rodriguez; William Roesch; Mr. and Mrs. Edward Roesler; J. Hugh Roff Jr.; Bud and Suzanne Rogers; William Rogers; Felix Rohatyn; Sevesa Roko; John Romeo; Larry and Joni Rosenberg; Bob Rosengarten; Janie Rosenthal; Graham and Helen Ross; Bertha Roth; Wanda Rotz; Abdelkader Rouchdi; Tineka Rougier; Bob Rowan; Charlie Rowe; Harry Rozyn; Howard Rudnitsky; Florence Rudulph; Bob and Martha Frances Russell; Jim and Jane Russo; Bonner Rust; Nick and Nancy Rutgers; Derald and Janet Ruttenberg; Larry Rutter; Jim Ryder; Marie Ryder; Ellie Ryland; Errol and Jean Ryland; Ty Ryland; Dick Sabine; Dave Sacks; Kris and Katie Saitoh; Jona Sakaelevu; Ed Sakalian; Matilda Saladrau; Marcos Salas; Cynthia Saltzman; Tadeo Samate; Joe and Tillie Sanchez; Marc Sanders; David and Jane Sargent; John Sargent; Len and Sandy Sargent; Bob and Anna Sarnoff; Ralph and Bette Saul; Bob and Molly Saunders; Dero and Bea Saunders; Harris and Jean Saunders; Meli Savubuluti; John Sawhill; Tenn Schad; Frank Schaffer; Paul Schaffer; Peter Schaffer; Ray Schaffer; Harvey Schein; Paul and Rose Schierl; David Schiff; John Schiff; Walter and Dorothy Schirmer; Ken and Sissie Schley; Reeve and Lib Schley; Reeve and Georgie Schley; Herb Schlosser; Bill Schmick; Chauncey Schmidt; Peter and Abby Schoff; John Schork; Ron and Dede Schue; Rey and Hedi Schwab; Sylvia Schwartz; David Scott; George and Myra Scott; Scotty and Loradein Scott; Buzzy and Joan Scribner; Charlie Scribner; Bob and Naomi Scrivener; Jack and Liz Seabrook; Bill Seale; Bill and Judy Seawell; Tod and Kate Sedgwick; Harry and Consuelo Seherr-Thoss; Ann Seif; Jan Seitz; Suluka Sekaia; Dick Sellers; Harry Seneker; Mohamed Serghini; Tevita Sesina;

Phyllis Sestan; George Sexton; Irving Shapiro; Bob Sharbaugh; Jesse Shaver; Kathleen Shea; Marylou Sheils; Ruth Shelton; Shep Shepard; Mark Shepherd; Jim Shepley; Jim Sheridan; Bob Shevlin; Dick and Helen Shinn; George and Sammie Shinn; Jane Shioshita; Charles Shirk; Nasser Shirzad; Win and Janet Short; Eileen Shump; Ruth Shump; Forrest and Patsy Shumway; Andy and Peggy Sigler; Mr. and Mrs. Ramon H. Silton; Herb Silverman; Nancy Simmons-Christie; Hank Simon; Harold Simon; Norton and Jennifer Simon; John Simpson; Al and Barrie Singer; Bob and Audrey Six; Ambassador Ali Skalli; Connie Skeeter; Hank Slack; Tom and Jackie Slaughter; Ed Slegers; Hank and Irene Slegers; Bruce Smart; Irwin Smiley; Bertha Smith; Fred Smith; Geof Smith; Stan and Elaine Smith; Mary Smith; Phil and Sheila Smith; Ward Smith; Alan Snart; Bill Sneath; Ambassador Ahmed Snoussi; Kenneth Snowman; Therese Snyder; Anna Sofus; Lew Solomon; Steve Solomon; Ben Sonnenberg; Doug Song; Deke Sonnichsen; Ralph Sorenson; Ken and Irene Soubry; Arlen Southern; Clancy and Ginnie Spangle; Bob Sparks; Bill Spencer; Ed and Harriet Spencer; Jo Spencer; Neal Spencer; Bonnie Spohr; Jim Spring; King and Sissy Sprott; Steve Stamas; John and Valerie Stanger; Louis and Abbey Starr; Ogden and Pat Starr; Andy Stasiak; Bud and Diley Staub; Don Steele; Karl and Lucy Stefan; Howard Stein; Eric Steinhardt; Bob Sterenson; Augustus Sterne; Jim Stickney; Jack Stine; Charles Stinson; Mr. and Mrs. Prentice Stout; Bob Strack; Bill and Janet Strauss; Jim and Judy Streeter; George and Sandi Strichman; Paul Sturm; Fred and Judi Sullivan; Gene Sullivan; John Sullivan; Arthur and Lynn Sultan; Punch Sulzberger; Edward Surren; Gordon and Alta Sweany; Barrie Sweetman; Captain Albert Sylvia; Margaret Symonds; Bill and Arlene Taggart; Peni Tagutu; Al and Odette Tahmoush; Seiichi Takikawa; Marion Talmage; Prent and Sybie Talmage; Ed and Mary Tan; Fred Taylor; Jim and Margaret Taylor; Bob Templin; Mohamed Sahraoui Terraf; John and Susan Terry; Walter and Grace Terry; Paul and Margery Thayer; Lowell Thomas; Pen Thomas; Ralph Thomas; Joyce Thompson; Tim and Ruth Thompson; Hugh Thomson; Norma Thomson; Charlie Thorn; Bill and Ria Thornton; John Thornton; Tex Thornton; Judy Tigges; Filipe Tiko; Timoci Tikoimaleya; Waisele Tila; Robin Tilney; Jim and Mary Tinsley; Web and Eleanor Todd; Janet Toenniessen; Alberto and Pia Togni; Kamieli Tola; President and Mrs. William Tolbert; John and Anne Torell; Nap and Ann Torpey; Jim and Virginia Towey; Beth

Tracy; John Train; Jerry Trautman; Curt and Earline Troeger; Regina Trudell; Ron Trujillo; Donald J. Trump; M. Tui; Bob and Mary Agnes Tullis; Dick and Chaille Tullis; Ambassador Leo Tuominen; Bill and Betty Turnbull; Jake and Olga Turner; Cliff Tweter; Lila Tyng; Marianne Tyrrasch; Allyson Tyson; Don Uhlenhopp; Apaitia Ulutegu; Dick Unwin; Ed Utermohle; George Valentine; Isaac Ben Valentine; Richard Valentine; Alejandro and Conchita Vallecillo; Amy Vance; Spider and Gay Vance; Gracie Vance; E. J. Van Cleft; Mme. Vandenberghe; Henry Van Der Eb; Bob Van Fossan; Alice Van Orden; Cary Van Pelt; Feitze Van Zwol; Manasa Vaquera; George and Marvel Vaughan; Tink Veale; Arnold Veevers; Bash Veghte; Vilimore Vegunu; Bunny Veit; Joseva Velo; Vera Vent; Tsikia Verebula; Joe Vergara; Bill and Peggy Verity; Qalo Vesuki; Frank Vigil; Blair Villa; Diana Villa; Nick Villa; Peter Villa; Tony Villa; Tony and Di Villa; Wendy Villa; Bob and Joan Vivian; Chuck Vogeley; Alvin Vogtle; Bob and Barbara Volk; Franz von Bayern; Hans and Evelyn von Becker; Kolja von Bismarck; Fritz and Stephanie von Bismarck-Osten; Mathias von Bismarck-Osten; Arnulf and Cordula von Heyl; Cornelius von Heyl; Cornibert and Marianne von Heyl; Hilda-Marie von Heyl; Ulrich and Anne von Heyl; Willie von Meister; Carl-Ludwig von Schlabrendorff; Jurgen-Lewin and Beate von Schlabrendorff; Moritz von Schlabrendorff; Cort and Ade Voorhees; Kent and Lisa Voorhees; Sitiveni Vueti; Samisoni Vugakoto; Ambassador and Mrs. B. Vunibobo; Page and Betty Wadsworth; Titch and Allen Wagner; Janet Waked; Al and Audrey Walan; Hicks and Evelyn Waldron; Eton Walker; Henry and Nancy Walker; Walter Walla; DeWitt and Lila Wallace; Kelly Waller; Gordon Wallis; Paul Walter; Susan Walter; Barbara Walters; Arthur and Mary Ellen Wang; Jude Wanniski; Terry Ward; Les and Mary Warner; Rawleigh Warner; Jack Washburn; Hermione Waterfield; Julian and Priscilla Wathen; Eve Watson; Jeannette Watson; Stuart and Jane Watson; Tom and Olive Watson; Gurdon and Peter Wattles; Bill and Jane Wearly; Rosemary Webber; Ben Weberman; Ken Weddelton; John Weinberg; Gertrude Weiner; Fred Weisman; Wayne Welch; Ralph Weller; His Grace the Duke of Wellington; Fred Wellington; Orson Welles; Don Welsh; Jann Wenner; Bo and Ginna Wentworth; Canon Edward West; Eric and Jeannie West; Steve and Ann West; Josh Weston; Harry and Maggie Wetzel; Peggy Whelan; Eileen White; Graham and Gabrielle Whitehead; John Whitehead; Dale Whitman; Denise Wiederkehr; Donna

Wiederkehr; Matt and Bobbie Wiederkehr; Kathy Wiegner; Cheryl Wiesenfeld; Jennie Wighton; Tom Wilcox; Spencer and Louisa Wilking; Larry and Phyl Wilkinson; Thomas Willers; Harold Williams; Marc and Bella Williams; Richard Williams; Dick and Kate Wilson; John Wilson; Elizabeth Winn; John and Anne Winston; Lee Winston; John Winthrop; Bill and Boopy Wister; Bill and Christene Witter; Chris and Grace Witting; Peter Wodtke; Charles and Rose Wohlstetter; Charlie and Helen Woodman; Bob Woodruff; Walt Wriston; Dolores Wurtzel; Dan Wynn; Inoke Yabaki; Bonnie Yablon; Len and Cacky Yablon; Scott and Patty Yablon; Ray Yavneh; Josefa Yaya; Lise Yellis; Bill and Janey Ylvisaker; Ted York; Fred Young; Ed Yost; Habih Younis; Marie Zacarese; Ambassador Ardeshir Zahedi; Nasser Zahedi; Shelly Zalaznick; Peggy Zalecki; Roger Zapke; Betsy Zavell; Mary Ann Zlatnik; George and Sue Zipf; Don Zipperer; Jessica Dee Zive; Abdeslam Zouadi; Lothar zu Dohna.

Contents

Introduction

It's oft been said that if something is worth saying, it's worth the effort required to say it in as few words as possible. I agree with that observation much more than I practice it. Brevity is far more than the source of wit. It's the font of wisdom.

For several of *Forbes* magazine's six decades, one of the regular features my founding father wrote in every issue was a column called "Two Line Editorials." He often observed that they were far harder to do than the lengthier, opinionated pages of "Fact and Comment."

The thoughts presented here have occurred and been put to paper at odd times more than at scheduled writing hours, sometimes in the middle of the night by penlight to avoid wifely ire, but more often after a dinner drink or two (a fact alluded to in a few).

Whether these are labeled Thoughts, Epigrams, Maxims, Observations, Truths, Comments or whatever doesn't much matter. If some ring a bell or trigger a reader's reaction, stimulate a response, that's all that matters.

Too often, clear thinking and ideas worth expressing get buried in verbiage. Meaningful truths are never newly discovered; they're just uncovered anew. Ponderousness and pomposity burden rather than brighten the mind. That's for sure not what we have in mind here.

I hope you have a fraction of the fun in reading a few of these that I had in writing them.

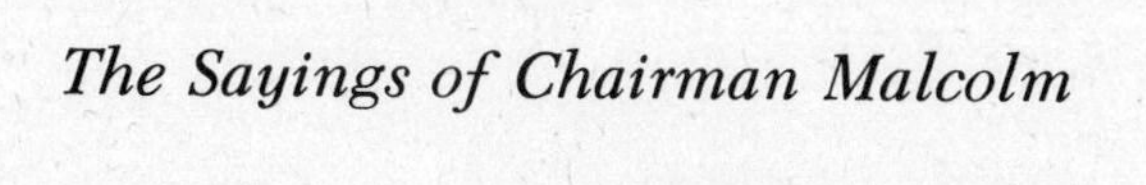

The Sayings of Chairman Malcolm

Eye-Openers

LOVE

is a positive charge—if your battery isn't dead.

A BORE

Someone who persists in holding to his
own views
after we have enlightened him with ours.

THE HARDEST WORK OF ALL

Doing nothing.

NEVER SAY DIE

until you've done it.

ONE GROUP OF DOCTORS WHO STILL MAKE HOUSE CALLS

Coroners.

Reaching High

HOW WOULD YOU KNOW WHAT HAPPY IS
if you'd never been otherwise?

CONTRARY TO THE CLICHÉ
genuinely nice guys most often
finish first or very near it.

PUTTING PEN TO PAPER
lights more fires than matches ever will.

INSPIRATION
and perspiration are related by more
than rhyme.

PRETENSE
invariably impresses only the pretenders.

TOO FEW
accomplish twice as much as too many.

THERE ARE MORE FAKERS
in business than in jail.

THOSE WHO TALK LOUDLY
are rarely listened to.

LIVING AND DREAMING
are two different things—but you can't do one without the other.

FULFILLING DESIRES
is less rewarding than pursuing 'em.

IF YOU'VE NEVER FAILED
you won't succeed.

WHY BOTHER?
When you don't want something enough to make *the* effort, making *an* effort is a waste.

BETTER IS BETTER

Some people as a result of adversity
are sadder, wiser, kinder, more human.
Most of us are better, though, when
things go better.
All good poets didn't and don't
necessarily need garrets.

WHEN YOU CAN'T CHANGE

don't fret.

WHAT YOU CAN'T CHANGE

don't sweat.

FULFILLMENT

If you expect nothing, you're apt
to be surprised.
You'll get it.

BEING LITTLE BELITTLES

Keeping score of old scores and scars,
getting even and one-upping always make
you less than you are.

IN BUSINESS
too sharp is seldom smart.

ONCE IN A WHILE
there's wisdom in recognizing that
the Boss is.

DON'T WORRY
As has been oft observed, most of
the things we worry most about don't
happen.
So—
Don't.

ABILITY
will never catch up with the demand
for it.

IF YOU DON'T KNOW
what you want to do,
it's harder to do it.

THE UNDRIVEN
don't get there.

STAND TALL

The difference between towering and cowering is totally a matter of inner posture. It's got nothing to do with height.

It costs nothing.

And it's much more fun.

IF YOU CAN DO

don't not.

TRYING TO IMPRESS OTHERS

does—usually in quite a negative way.

HOW TO SUCCEED

Try hard enough.

HOW TO FAIL

Try too hard.

FLAVOR

Unsuccess sours the sharp and mellows the able.

YOU PAY FOR EVERYTHING

Including even speaking your mind (with or without one).

Why is it that speaking your mind (or writing it) tees off so vehemently all those who can't or won't or don't?

BEING TOO WELL UNDERSTOOD

motivates most who complain about being misunderstood.

MANY MAY KNOW LITTLE

but most sense much.

WE ALL LIKE TO BE ASKED

even if we say no.

OBSERVATION

Those who act as if they know more than their boss seldom do.

Those who do, have sense enough not to make it obvious—to the boss.

NO, NEVER
I've learned never to use the word never, because there's no such thing.

IF & WHEN YOU ARE QUALIFIED
to give advice, it's because you rarely took it.

NEVER LET TURNDOWNS
get you down.

TOO MANY PEOPLE
overvalue what they're not and undervalue what they are.

IF YOU HAVE A JOB
without any aggravations, you don't have a job.

SOMETIMES DOING WHAT'S EXPECTED
is more effective than doing the unexpected.

THE REAL JOY
is in the contemplation.

VENTURE NOTHING
and life is less than it should be.

NO WINNER
always is.

VICTORY IS SWEETEST
when you've known defeat.

PLAN ACCORDINGLY
The only immutability is change.

OBSERVATION
Those who enjoy responsibility usually get it; those who merely like exercising authority usually lose it.

IT'S ALWAYS WORTHWHILE
to make others aware of their worth.

IF YOU SAY WHAT YOU THINK
don't expect to hear only what you like.

ONE THING THAT PREVIOUS PRACTICE DOESN'T ALWAYS MAKE PERFECT

Marriage.

CONSOLATION

If you've had a good time playing the game, you're a winner even if you lose.

BOWDLERIZING ROBBY BURNS

Never try to appear to be what you want to be.

Either be what you want to be or be as you are.

PETER'S PRINCIPLE, PERHAPS, NOT MINE

People are talking about the new "civilized" way to fire executives. You kick 'em upstairs.

They're given a title, a liberal tithe, nothing to do, and a secretary to do it with.

What a way to go!

WHEN YOU START TO THINK

that you deserve your blessings, you don't.

RE: SUDDEN SHUFFLES IN EXECUTIVE SUITES
It's 10 A.M. Do you know where *your* board of directors is?

THERE IS A DIFFERENCE
between getting what you pay for
and what you hope for.

GOLF LINK
Drivers go further than putterers.

KNOWING WHEN TO KEEP YOUR MOUTH SHUT
is invariably more important than opening it at the right time.

THOSE WHO CAN'T FORGET
what should be are self-cripplers.

THE ULTIMATE IN OPTIMISM
Confidence that there is no next world.

HONORS
are easier had than honor.

THE LONG AND THE SHORT OF IT
In the long run, a short cut
seldom is.

PEOPLE WHO CAN'T SEE
without glasses should wear them.

YOU TOO CAN BE A GURU
Do you know any Belief or Faith
with followers that doesn't have
as its foundation the Golden Rule?

THERE'S NO WAY TO MOVE
without making waves.

ALWAYS LISTEN TO A MAN
when he describes the faults of others.
Ofttimes, most times, he's describing
his own, revealing himself.

THE ULTIMATE HIGH
A man's abilities equaling his
opinion of 'em.

SURVIVAL
Few survive success too soon.

NEVER DENIGRATE
what you should appreciate.

DREAMS
are not meant to be realized.

LISTENING TO ADVICE
often accomplishes far more than heeding it.

IF YOU CAN READ AND DON'T
you're dumb.

WE'D ALL LIKE TO BE TAKEN
for what we'd like to be.

WHEN WHAT WE ARE
IS WHAT WE WANT TO BE
that's happiness.

If It's a Big Think, Begin at the End

Over the years, I've evolved a somewhat heretical but real time- and mind-saving approach to books, articles, editorials that deal with weighty matters.

More often than not, by beginning at the end and contemplating the conclusions, one can determine if it's worth going through the whole to get there.

Arrived

THE TOP PEOPLE OF THE BIGGEST COMPANIES
are, surprisingly, often the nicest ones in their company. I'm not sure, though, if they got there because they were good guys or that they're now good guys because they can afford to be.

BOSS THOUGHTS
You can't know if no one tells you.
You can't answer the question if no one asks it.
You can't solve the problem if no one poses it.

NEVER HIRE SOMEONE
who knows less than you do about what he's (or she's) hired to do.

PEOPLE WHO DON'T KNOW EVERYTHING THAT EVERYBODY PRESUMES THEY DO

Tycoons.

AT THE HEART

of any good business is a chief executive officer with one.

NOTE TO SALARY SETTERS

Pay your people the least possible and you'll get from them the same.

THE BEST BUY

by way of management is brains—at any price.

THE LONG AND THE SHORT OF IT

An inadequate chief executive officer's time at the top is always too long no matter how short. The right CEO's reign invariably seems too short no matter how long.

WHEN IN DOUBT

duck.

DEPARTURE IS SUCH SWEET NEWS
for those a-waiting.

IT FIGURES
People whose values are the least
make the most about the least.

THE SMART ONES ASK
when they don't know. And, sometimes,
when they do.

GOODBYE
When those with ability at their
job get to thinking they can't be
done without, they're really on their
way.
Out.

BEING RIGHT HALF THE TIME
beats being half right all the time.

WHEN PROFIT IS UNSHARED
it's less likely to grow greater.

MOST OLDSTERS
are fascinated by the Future, while the young love to look back to earlier days, especially their own.

HOW ABOUT YOU?
When looking back, usually I'm more sorry for the things I didn't do than for the things I shouldn't have done.

SECURITY
isn't securities.
It's knowing that someone cares whether you are or cease to be.

ASSURANCE
reassures.

TO HAVE A BIG POT
you have to be rich.

NOTHING
is sometimes the right thing to say.

EXECUTIVES WHO GET THERE AND STAY suggest solutions when they present the problems.

Those who don't, don't.

GREAT COINAGE

I heard one Wheel describe another:

"He's absolutely copeless."

STANDARD

You can easily judge the character of others by how they treat those who can do nothing for them or to them.

SIZE AND TIME

Small (minded) people don't long run big companies.

TO BE AGREEABLE

while disagreeing—that's an art.

THOSE WHO DON'T MATTER

will eventually be—along with those who do.

TO GROW OLD AND STILL BE LOVED

Be kind and sweet,
good and gracious
—and have something to
bequeath.

HOPELESS CASES

Executives who assert themselves
by saying No when they should say
Yes.

AUTHORITY'S FOR SHARING

only when the sharer is sure of his (or hers).

IT'S THE LESS-BRIGHT STUDENTS

who make teachers teach better.

TOP CATS

are often former underdogs who didn't like it.

CLOUT

is something some seem to have—
until they try exercising it.

THOSE CARRIED AWAY BY POWER
are soon carried away. Might of
the moment isn't a mite in Time.

HOW CAN YOU AVOID
people who say, "Let me tell you,"
and then do?

THOSE MOST SURE
they Have It, most usually haven't.

YOU HAVE TO BE OLD
before you can enjoy being young
in spirit.

THEORY OF CONTRARY OPINION
Sometimes,
the longer you live,
the more you live.

THE ULTIMATE IN SEDATIVES
At the first hello, the person who
made it telling you how.

NO ONE'S A LEADER
if there are no followers.

POINT
Those in the know, know that knowing all is unlikely.

THE HARDEST TIME TO TELL
When to stop.

A WORLD OF DIFFERENCE
In business, there's such a thing as the invaluable person, but no such thing as an indispensable one.

AVOIDING OR MUTING CRISES
is often far better than precipitating such.

HE WHO HESITATES
is sometimes wise.

ONCE YOU'VE GIVEN ADVICE
to someone, you're obligated.

TARGETS MUST BE VISIBLE
You have to come up in the world
before it's worthwhile for those
worth less to put you down.

SMOOTHING ROUGH SPOTS
sometimes requires abrasives.

IT DEPENDS ON WHERE YOU'RE AT
Elders always lament change—
and the young cannot wait for it.

WHEN YOU DON'T UNDERSTAND
it's sometimes easier to look like you do.

BY THE TIME
we make it.
we've had it.

PEOPLE IN THEIR FORTIES
are either oatsy (on the verge of Having
It Made) or sudsy (realizing and
explaining why they ain't).

RIGHT?
All work and no play makes jack.
With enough jack, Jack needn't be a dull boy.

WHEN THE JOY OF THE JOB'S GONE,
when it's no fun trying anymore,
quit before you're bounced.

NONE MESS UP MORE OFTEN
than the old—except the young.

FROM HIGH ALTITUDES
and high-'n'-mighty attitudes,
dizziness results.

IT'S GREAT
to Arrive, but the trip's most
always most of the fun.

The Next Century-The Year 2000

Sounds like a long way off, doesn't it?

On the other hand, for some of us it seems like yesterday when Ike was in the White House, the U.S. Senate censured Joe McCarthy, and the Supreme Court unanimously ruled that racial segregation in public schools was unconstitutional.

Yet that was hardly more than a couple dozen years ago.

And the next century's only a few years away.

Simple Truths

WHEN THINGS ARE BAD
we take a bit of comfort in the thought that they could always be worse. And when they are, we find hope in the thought that things are so bad they have to get better.

THE ART OF CONVERSATION
lies in listening.

TO LISTEN
often is to obligate.

TO MEASURE THE MAN
measure his heart.

IF YOU DON'T KNOW
it's not always necessary to admit it.

WANT-GIVE

If you want understanding, try
giving some.

ONE THING'S FOR SURE

in this bewildering, uncertain business climate. As prices of the things they buy continue climbing faster than take-home pay, consumers have no choice but to consume less and less of more and more.

LOOKING THE PART

helps get the chance to fill it.

IF YOU FILL THE PART

it matters not if you look it.

FUNNY ISN'T IT

how it's always Out to want to be In.

WITH APOLOGIES TO ROBERT BURNS

O wad some Pow'r the giftie gie us
to be loved as well
by those we love so well.

GENEROUS GESTURES
yield the most when that isn't their purpose.

SELF-SYMPATHY
Hoarding one's hurts hurts only the hoarder.

UNNEW THOUGHT
Givers get while takers put.

GIVE NAUGHT
get same.

GIVE MUCH
get same.

IT'S SO MUCH EASIER
to be enthusiastic—especially when there's grounds for it.

WORKING AT WHAT YOU ENJOY
is far more important than what you're working at.

FAILURE IS SUCCESS
if we learn from it.

A BRAIN UNUSED
is like a fallow field.
If it's resting, that's good.
If it's rotting, that's bad.
If you have one, use it.

WHICH ART IS MOST RARE?
One often reads about the art of conversation—how it's dying or what's needed to make it flourish, or how rare good ones are. But wouldn't you agree the infinitely more valuable rara avis is a good listener?

THE DUMBEST PEOPLE
I know are those who Know It All.

WHOEVER COINED THE PHRASE
"smart ass" has got to be at least half right.

THINKERS PERISH
Thoughts don't.

ONE WHO NEVER ASKS
either knows everything or nothing.

A GOOD HEART
can no more be concealed than a bad one.

A HUG'S A HAPPY THING
while a shrug's so often destructive.

EXCEPTIONS
There are no exceptions to the rule that everybody likes to be an exception to the rule.

IT'S VERY FLATTERING
to ask others about matters
they're little qualified to discuss.

IF YOU'RE LOOKING
for perfection, look in the mirror.
If you see it there, expect it elsewhere.

MORE OFTEN THAN NOT
things and people are as they appear.

IT FIGURES

Thin people are thin fare if their figure's their principal concern.

TO REVEAL

attempt to conceal.

A CONTRADICTION IN TERMS

Mini skirt under maxi coat.

COMPLIMENT OTHERS

on the virtues they have and they're not half as pleased as being complimented for having the ones they don't have.

THE ULTIMATE IN FUTILITY

Owning "important" jewelry. Insurers often insist on the wearing of paste replicas because necks with real rocks around 'em risk wringing.

WITH CARDS, CANDY, AND OTHER THINGS

Why is it that the one you want is always on the bottom?

IT'S SO MUCH EASIER
to suggest solutions when you don't know too much about the problem.

HELP
He who says he never needs help, most does.

WHEN ONE SEEKS ASSURANCE
there's none from those who respond, "Now, don't you worry about a thing." If you weren't worried, you wouldn't have asked. If you are concerned, it's nice to know that those you query are, too.

I'll take a worrier any day over a platitudinous reassurer.

TO BE TOO INNOCENT
is both dumb and dangerous.

WHEN IT'S YOUR OWN FAULT
things hurt worse than when there's someone else to blame.

TRUST
and you'll elicit trust.

YOU'RE FORTUNATE
when you can afford to be virtuous.

THINGS THERE ARE NO SOLUTIONS TO
Inflation, bureaucracy & dandruff.

WHEN THE MOOD MOVES YOU
move with it.

HOW TO GET TAKEN
Spend most of your time being sure
you're not.

MOST EVERYONE WANTS TO DO
what's fair, right, and good, but knowing
what is is often the tough part.

IT'S BETTER TO BE FEARFUL
than fear filled.

FIRST COUSINS

Common sense and experience.
One leads to the other.
Usually.

CAR DOORS

Unless you're always only two, or lean
and young,
four doors doubly beats two.

SHORT AND SMALL

It doesn't take much of a rule
to measure a mean man.

ONE OF THE CEASELESS WONDERS OF THE WORLD

The power of a smile.

SCIENTISTS OFTTIMES HAVE THE GREATEST FAITH

in a higher power.

The more they dig into, establish facts and figures, the more they marvel at the mystery of it all.

QUESTION

Since we had nothing to do with our Arrival and usually are not consulted on our Departure, what makes so many of us think we're entitled to so much while we're here?

PEOPLE WHO STARE

deserve the looks they get.

THE GOOD GUYS ADMIRE

while the bad guys envy.

ARE YOU NOT JUSTIFIED IN FEELING INFERIOR

when you seek to cover it with arrogance and insolence?

THE ONLY THING NEVER MISPLACED

Consideration.

TWO KINDS

Food may be essential as fuel for
the body, but good food is fuel for
the soul.

UNLESS YOU'RE SERVING TIME
there's never enough of it.

THE MYTHIQUE
about wine is half the fun.
The other two-thirds is the taste.
And the remaining three-fourths comes from adequate imbibition.

TITLES
only entitle the holders to live up, in appearance at least, to relevant expectations.

TALKING ABOUT PROBLEMS OF OVERPOPULATION
How 'n heck are they handling their surplus in Hell these days? Maybe by the time you and I are in the queue, there won't be room for us.

THE ONLY UNFORGIVABLE SIN
Being unforgiving.

IT'S MORE FUN TO ARRIVE
at a conclusion than to justify it.

IF YOU DON'T
watch your figure,
you'll have more figure to watch.

IF YOU LIVE LIFE FEARFULLY
you'll die many times before the finals.

WHEN YOU CAN'T SLEEP
you dream of it.

WHEN YOU CEASE TO DREAM
you cease to live.

INEVITABLE CYCLE
After the facts, our hearts invariably go out to the fallen Goliaths.
Yet we invariably root for their Davids.
Until they're winners.

THE DIFFERENCE BETWEEN MEN AND BOYS
is in the price of their toys.

MOST PEOPLE ARE
what they say they're not.

CONTRARY OPINION
Making mistakes is human.
Repeating 'em is too.

PALETTE AND TASTE
make for good art, meals, and sex.

ADVICE
It's more fun to give than to receive.

ATTENTION
is more fun to get than to give.

ACCEPTING BLAME
when it's not really due
sometimes makes the point better.

ADDRESSING SOMEONE AS "DEARIE"
is not endearing.

ANY MARRIAGE THAT SURVIVES A BIG WEDDING
can probably survive.

ARRIVING

for an appointment or a luncheon or a dinner engagement an hour late is almost as bad as arriving an hour early.

AFTER FORTY

one's face begins to tell more than one's tongue.

DRINKING

more often brings out the best in the good
than the worst in the bad.

LONELINESS

is the worst—
aloneness too long is impossible.
To be is to need and be needed by others.

LIFE

Everything's relative.
Joy is a state of mind vis-à-vis sadness.
You can't have one without the other.
And would we want it any other way?
No—when you've got sadness.
Yes—when you've got joy.

"Personal & Confidential"

Letters so marked should be.

Many executives to whom they are addressed open such themselves—after all, they might be from an old girl friend or contain stuff that might make savvy secretaries sassy.

When the contents are only printed matter, though, the minifrauder succeeds in sowing ill will and ire.

Definitions

OFF-BROADWAY THEATER
Usually offal.
(As bad as that; sometimes verse.)

INVESTOR
One who bought stocks that went up.

SPECULATOR
One who bought stocks that went down.

A PARDON
is a forgiveness, not a reward.

PASSÉ
Whatever's the In Thing by the time
you and I hear of it.

A WINNER
must first know what losing's like.

DISTANT RELATIONS
Theory and practice.

WANTING & WANTON,
THE DIFFERENCE BETWEEN
is in the spelling.

MIRRORS
People who think people are jerks, are.

UNFULFILLING
Fulfilled desires.

PLEASURE
is more in contemplation than
realization.

PATTER
A wonderful means of avoiding the Matter.

ASTROLOGY

isn't something I'm into, but while awaiting the transatlantic balloon attempt, the *Los Angeles Times* Jan. 1, 1975 column on the subject under my sign, Leo, advised:

"Find cheaper and faster forms of transportation."

WHAT IS INFLATION?

Taxation.

Nothing more, nothing less.

It's the devastating price of the Free Lunch.

WIZARD

It takes one to know there are none.

UNNECESSARY PEOPLE

Those who are necessary so that the necessary people can know they are.

VENOM

Invaluable.

But only as an antidote to snakebite.

MEANNESS

Demeans the demeaner far more than the demeaned.

JACKASSES

are hard to disguise.

WHAT DO YOU CALL A MUSCULAR SPIRITUAL ADVISER?

A gurulla.

PHONINESS

is such hard work (that's an observation, not a confession).

WHO ARE YOU?

Sometimes, who you think you are.

CAFÉ SOCIETY

Where it's important to Matter for those who don't to those who don't.

DEFINITION OF NICE PEOPLE

People who are nice to us.

THOSE WHO KNOW IT ALL
know nothing.

GOOD HEALTH
is the realest wealth.

WORD PLAY
To maintain a posture requires posturing, which suggests imposture.
Where does one begin and the other end?

EGO TRIPS
trip.

LEISURE SUITS
suit neither function.

CHINESE PROVERB
Girl with little behind and lot in front
has assured future.

PEOPLE
who live their lives to impress
others, do neither.

THE MOST USEFUL PIECE OF OFFICE EQUIPMENT

A wastebasket.

AGE

marinates those who live long enough
to have some.

Whether one ends up a cynic or a wise man depends on the seasoning added along the way.

SO

Clichés are because they're so.

A MATURE PERSON

One who agrees with you.

ART

is what to you it is.

COMMON SENSE

is a most uncommon quality.

The Rites of Spring

Trees send Joyce Kilmer, but nothing quite sends most Americans like the smell of a new car interior and the soul-satisfying sound of shutting a new car door.

There are few among us who don't find that sound as exciting as a bar of music. There are few among us who do not put a new chariot's aroma on a par with the perfume of the loveliest blooms. It's a deep yearning for both of these that, at this time of year, drives so many to the nearest automobile showroom. Call it what you want, or call for the psychiatrist, but it's a powerful fact of American life.

Nobody's Capitalist Fool!

"MONEY ISN'T EVERYTHING"
According to those who have it.

ONE WONDERFUL FREEDOM
Being free, and able to afford to make one's own mistakes.

PEOPLE WHO KNOCK MONEY
either have too much or too little.
Most can't get enough of it.

ENOUGH
is measurable.

ENOUGH IS ENOUGH
of what, and who says?

WHAT'S THE ANSWER TO 99 OUT OF 100 QUESTIONS?
Money.

COSTLESS HIGH
There are more kicks in doing someone good than in doing someone in.

SOCIALISM WILL BE HERE
the day we share our profits to the degree we share our failures.

I GUESS IT'S GOOD
That people almost never regret having bought the things they couldn't afford.

THERE'S A BIG DIFFERENCE
between cheap and reasonable.

BY BEING TOO SHARP
in buying, you cut yourself along with the price.

TO LEAD A FULL, RICH LIFE
money helps. To lead a merely rich life,
money ruins.

INFLATION FOOTNOTE
I remember when, at dime-a-dance-
hall, tickets were ten cents
apiece.

IT ISN'T ALWAYS ADVANTAGEOUS
to deprive one's children of
disadvantages.

OFTEN
You pay less when you pay more.

IF IT'S GOOD
too little is always far better
than too much.

ONE THING TO BE SAID
FOR INHERITED MONEY
It beats not having any.

WHEN ONE IS DESCRIBED AS "RICH"
it's always well to ask, "In what?"

THE LINE BETWEEN
idiosyncrasy and idiocy is Money.

THEY CAN AFFORD IT
People who are the Most
demand the Least.

THERE ARE MORE HUSTLERS IN BUSINESS
than on street corners.

IT'S NICE
when people have enough money to consider
the stuff unimportant.

IF YOU CAN
pay your way.

IF YOU WANT TO
and can,
do.

A COMPANY WITH MORE CASH THAN IT NEEDS
more often than not uses it in such a way as to reverse the problem.

MANY ECONOMISTS ARE GOING TO BRAZIL
to learn the inflation carioca—it has a beat they'd like to beat.

MONEY'S WORTH
Payment in kindness beats by a thousand times the pleasure of payment in kind.

REAL RICHES
are measured to one's degree of freedom—freedom to do or not to do, to think or not to think, to be or not to be. Having money helps one to be free, but not if getting it costs more than what one wants it for.

THOSE WHO HAVE IT
don't need to assert it.

THOSE WHO HAVE IT
don't need to flaunt it.

ALWAYS
Be willing to pay dear for what you hold dear.

PEOPLE'S WEALTH AND WORTH
are very rarely related.

INDEPENDENCE IS A TWO-LEGGED THING
For one to be independent, political freedom is a first essential.

The other essential's a job—bucks in the bank.

SUCCESS
undiluted, undoes.

WHEN YOUR CUP RUNNETH OVER
turn off the tap.

IT'S NEVER A GOOD DEAL
when only one party thinks it is.

BEING GRABBY
makes such businesses and people grubby.

IT TAKES MONEY

Only the inordinately rich can afford unbridled pessimism.

The rest of us must look for silver linings in the blackest clouds.

WHAT A WAY TO BUY

Paying list price.

WHAT CAN'T BE SOLD

is usually sale-d.

SOMEONE WHO

"has everything" may—sometimes—have something.

THE MORE ONE HAS

to be modest about, the less one is likely to be.

JUST RICH CAN MEAN POOR

A life spent spending, empties more than your purse.

BLUE CHIPS
are what investors think they are.

MONEY IN THE BANK
means independence;
too much, dependence.

"MONEY IS A BURDEN"
Some of us are willing to shoulder
some burdens.

THERE'S NO SUCH THING
as paying the right people for the job
more than they're worth.

HARD WORK
Faking it.

MONEY'S FUN
when you have some.
Having none, ain't none.

MONEY
A means to the end.

Passing Parade

THE FIRST BORN

invariably has a tough time bringing up his parents.

If you have a choice, be last.

THE HEREAFTER

Those who know the answers never seem to be in a position to provide 'em.

THE DAY NOTHING TURNS YOU ON

You're dead.
No matter how many more years
you go on breathing.

NOSTALGIA NOTE

The other night I heard somebody order an old-fashioned.

THERE'S ONE THING
I always love about my birthday—
being around for it.

THAT'S LIFE
When you're an infant, you cannot be put down after feeding until you have burped. When you're older, everybody puts you down if you do.

CHILDREN MAY BE THE HOPE OF THE WORLD
but let's not get 'em too high (our hopes, that is). Just remember, our parents used to say the same thing about us. Now look.

SINCE YOU HAVE TO DO
the things you have to do, be wise enough
to do some of the things you want to do.

DELIGHTFUL REVERSE TWIST
I overheard at lunch two ageless elderly ladies discussing a third: "You know, my dear, she says she's 85 but I know she can't be over 79."

AGE

It should be a license, not a limitation.

TOUCHÉ

Concerning my editorial lament at reaching the age of 50, one friend suggested: "Don't complain. Think of the alternative."

SNORING

Anybody know a cure?

A MAN CAN'T

do more than he can—but he can at least do that much.

ON THE OTHER HAND

live less and you'll live longer.

LASTING EPHEMERALS

A good meal, a good deal, a good deed.

ONE THING LEADS TO ANOTHER

Like love and population.

THREE WORDS ALWAYS IN ORDER

Please
and
Thank you.

SAD—OR SENSIBLE?

I heard an older well-to-do woman say to another about her current escort: "He's available, attentive, and affectionate. At this stage in our lives, what more can we ask?"

RETIREMENT

works best for those who find the
most work to do.

FAMILY JOKE

Father: "May the Lord save me from being boring when I am old."
Son: "He's too late already."

WEIGHT

Mostly those who don't have the problem call attention to their weight. We who have it forbear from steering the conversation that weigh.

OLD AGE
is not for sissies.

HOW CHILDREN
survive being Brought Up amazes me.

OVERHEARD, ONE WEALTHY OLD LADY TO ANOTHER
"At our age, you have to keep your feet—they're so important."

WHEN OLD, YOU MIGHT AS WELL BE CHEERFUL
Who knows—in the next round you might have more reason to be dour.

TEMPUS FUGIT
So catch it if you can.

MORE AND MORE, THE YOUNG NO LONGER THINK
that real fulfillment is not having to fulfill any expectations.

TEARS OR CHEERS?

If growing old saddens you, then why cry for those who cease to?

WE CAN NEVER PAY

for all we're given.

WE WERE JOKING

with one of our unmarried sons who is in his late 20's about the fact that several of his more recent girlfriends have a child or two from failed marriages.

His rejoinder: "At this age some of the good ones are coming up again."

THE ONLY THING WORSE

than a smart kid is a dumb one.

IT'S SOMETIMES WELL TO REMEMBER

that life doesn't end when yours does.

I SO DIG LIVING

no one will be sadder when I'm dug under.

YOU'RE NEVER TOO OLD
until you admit it or are no longer
around to deny it.

RIGHT
No one wants to cease to matter
until he's ceased to be matter.

YOU HAVE TO BE OLDER
before you can enjoy
being young in spirit.

SPEAKING OF OLD-AGE CHEERFULNESS
reminds me of the story about the man who celebrated his 80th birthday by taking a bride of 18. Warned by his doctor that this was dangerous, he responded, "Well, if she dies, she dies."

THE ONLY THING MORE BORING
than doting parents is doting grandparents. My wife and I have just begun the latter role—with twins, yet.

OPTIMISM

For the young, it's natural.
For the old, it's a necessity.

MEDICAL ADVICE

If the doctor prescribes too tough a cure, change doctors.

WHEN YOU'RE 60

acting 30 fools only the actor.
It's more fun to be your age.

THERE'S A POPULAR SONG TITLED

"Times Ain't What They Used to Be."

No moment of time span for this Earth and the people on it has ever been or ever will be quite like the one before it.

And, aside from occasional moments of wistfully happy recollections, it's probably just as well.

IF YOU DON'T HAVE ALL THE ANSWERS

when you're under 21, you never will.

DEVOTING YOUR WHOLE LIFE TO YOUR CHILDREN can only burden and then bore 'em. When they're out of the nest, let 'em fly. Do your own thing, and let your young do theirs.

THE FUTURE

For the young, the future lies ahead.
For the Now age, the future is here.
For the old, the future is remembrance of things past.

JUST COMPENSATION, IS IT? that we grow more sensitive to slight lessons as life lengthens?

THE HIGH RATE OF DIVORCE among the country's young is not an indication of malaise in the generation. Rather it's a sign of hope.

If a marriage takes place and doesn't take, a take-out is more in order than pretense. Hypocrites are more often candidates for the Couch than those candidly recognizing mistakes.

LET YOUR CHILDREN GO
if you want to keep 'em.

THE ONLY THING
I'm going to ask for at my funeral is an air conditioner—with a long extension cord.

THE HARDEST THING
For those of us who are parents the most difficult thing asked by our young is not our earnings but our ears.

To hear 'em out before sounding off—ah, that's the test of whatever saintliness there might be in each or any of us.

INDICATIONS OF ONE'S AGE
Whenever more names on the obit page
are familiar.

KIDS IN THEIR EARLY TEENS
who don't regard their parents as an embarrassment or at best a nuisance, don't have proper parents.

IN MEMORIAM

That was a good man
said the worm.

GROWING CERTAINTY

Always remember to treat old folks
as you'd like to be if you were.
One day you might live so long, too.

WHERE IT'S AT

keeps changing or is never for long.

AGING ENTITLES ONE

to be tuckered, but not puckered.

LOOK-ALIKES

Have you ever noticed how many people long and harmoniously married get to look quite a lot alike? The next time you see a picture of a couple celebrating their fiftieth wedding anniversary, look at it closely and you'll see.

Most

Families

Have

an Auntie Mame–like aunt. Ours died not long ago at 84. She had a penchant for humorous asperity. Daily during her last days the doctor would list bits of unmeaningful "better symptoms." He recited a few just before her end. Aunt Kitty responded in a typical fashion: "Well, Doctor, you can tell the coroner I died of improvement.

Fact and Comment

WHO WANTS IT?

Can you imagine anything more stultifying than a perfect world populated entirely by problemless people?

That's what heavens are for.

PROPERLY ENTITLED

The other day a flattering letter arrived, addressed to the Ediotr-in-Chief. I prefer to think of it as a typographical error rather than a description.

BRITISH UNDERSTATEMENT EVER A DELIGHT

Found in Harrod's, London's huge and tony department store, is this civilized sign in elevators and elsewhere:

"Please Try Not To Smoke."

WHY IS SLEEPING LATE
most appealing when you can't?

TO EXORCISE THE DEVIL
Exercise like the devil.
That'll kill one of you.

ANSWERS
What good are they if there's no
question?

SIZE
Those who act Big seldom are.
True bigness is never capitalized.

UNTRUE TRUTH
"Neither a borrower nor a lender
be" may be sound advice, but what
a lonesome way to go through life.

QUESTION
Why should dishing it out have
any relationship to being able to take it?

SIGNS

So many signs seem to invite the action they forbid: Keep off the Grass, No Smoking, No Parking, and so forth.

But along the borders of a wild animal park that includes lions and the like, there's a sign that's apt to be observed: "Trespassers Will Be Eaten."

I guess sign results depend on what is said and how.

DENIM AND BLUE JEANS

The day will come when this stuff and these cease to be the only cloth and all clothes to almost all the populace . . . but don't hold your breath until then.

WHY DO SO MANY ROTUND LADIES

swaddle their ampleness in clinging
pants when cloaking their bounty would
be so much better?

SUGGESTED ADVERTISING SLOGAN
FOR AIRLINES

What a Way to Go!

ANYONE WHO SAYS BUSINESSMEN DEAL IN FACTS, NOT FICTION

has never read old five-year projections.

IF I SHOULD DIE

before I wake,
I pray the Lord our chef to take.

WHEN YOU NOTE THE SALARIES IN MANY NONPROFIT OUTFITS

it's no wonder so many go that route.

THE BOTTOM

If there's anything less attractive
than a girl chewing gum,
it's two girls chewing gum.

WHO ARE THEY FOOLING?

Public personalities who demand privacy
in public places.

GREAT ARCHITECTS ARE NO EXPENSE

except for accounting purposes;
what they build doesn't depreciate.

EVEN WORSE THAN KNOWING NOTHING

Recently I heard this observation attributed to one of Princeton's deans: ". . . he not only doesn't know anything—he doesn't even suspect anything."

At this same meeting, another educator observed about his course: "It's a difficult one, which I probably couldn't pass but can teach."

IF ONLY WE ALL COULD ANSWER THUS

Overheard in Schrafft's, one lady
to another, at the end of their meal:
"Are you financially balanced?"
The other: "No, I need about a dime."

SUSTAINING A THOUGHT

is harder than having one.

IF YOU HAVE A GOOD THOUGHT

grab it—there aren't too many flying around.

IF IT'S GOTTA BE A CHOICE

honest obtuseness is infinitely
preferable to dishonest astuteness.

HOW OVERBLOWN CAN YOU GET?

From the caption of an advertisement in *Antiques:*

"A Noteworthy Breakfront of Significant Importance."

JUDGE THYSELF

Would you rather commiserate or congratulate?

ALL WIVES

have the same problem—husbands.

But not having the problem can be a worse problem (husbands like to think).

SPEECHES AND WRITING

intended for Great Occasions often merely grate, always bore.

Since what most of us have to say is unapt to achieve immortality, we're wiser to leave Tablet prose to Moses.

THE MOST AUDIBLE RESULT OF WOMEN'S LIB

Men telephone operators.

A SMILE
increases your face value.
—Sign in a London shop.

SOLACING THOUGHT ON A BITTER COLD DAY
Enjoy shivering.
In the next life, we'll probably be complaining about the heat.

PEOPLE WHO NEVER GET CARRIED AWAY
should be.

IF IT'S
a big thing to you, what's wrong with making a Big Thing of it?

REPEATING MISTAKES
is more likely than profiting from them.

WHY IS IT
listeners always know when the speaker should stop and he seldom does?

WARNING: FORECASTS AHEAD

Aside from today's few *real* cowboys, the biggest bull-throwers around are economists.

What makes their salivating funniest isn't their wrongness—which exceeds that of weathermen—but the fact that they don't recognize it's bull they're throwing.

NEW WORDS TO AN OLD ARIA

O! solar mio.

OVERSIMPLIFICATION IS UNDERRATED

If oversimplification enables us to understand what we otherwise wouldn't grasp, it's a virtue.

ONLY DRIPS

drop out.

PEOPLE WHO MATTER

are most aware that everyone else does, too.

ONE'S FACE OFTTIMES SAYS

more than one's tongue.

BEING BORED IS BORING

When you are, you are to others.

WAY OUT

Ending editorials and articles with a question often enables one to avoid arriving at a conclusion.

IS OPEN-MINDEDNESS A VIRTUE?

I often think that when someone virtuously declares he has an "open mind," he's flattering an empty one.

UNLESS ONE'S RELIGION FORBIDS IT

don't you think it's selfish to die without leaving your body's useful parts to the living? After all, neither the worms nor the flames are short of material.

THERE MUST BE A MORAL SOMEWHERE

In the Good Old Days before Prohibition, there used to be a saloon on every corner.

Today there's a bank on every corner.

IN TAKEOVERS, NOTE HOW OFTEN
the Taken end up running the show.

AT THE RISK OF BEING BOMBED
I'd like to point out that Roman coffee is better than Irish.

THE ULTIMATE EGO TRIP
is a totally illegible signature.

DON'T YOU BELIEVE IT?
When somebody resorts to beginning his statements with the word "honestly," he's less likely to mean what he's saying.

AT BEAUTIFUL-PEOPLE EATERIES
most Beautiful People are more interested in chewing up each other than in what's on their plate.

ALWAYS HAND IN HAND
Prejudice and ignorance.
Cheapness and rudeness.

FAMILIARITY
breeds.

WHY IS IT
those with the least to say say it so much?

TO BE GOOD-LOOKING
is a handicap, it's often said—
usually by those who aren't.

WHY CAN'T SUMMER SUITS
ever hold their press?

QUERY
Why is it that those who pat their
own backs too hard give us and not
themselves a pain in the neck?

LIFE AND DEATH
You can't have one without the other.

WOULDN'T IT BE NICE
if everybody and everything were?
No.

WHERE IT'S AT
is seldom where it seems to be.

WHEN PEOPLE HAVE NOTHING
to do, they usually do it at the expense
of those who do.

CONSOLATION FOR CRITICS
Just because you throw stones, it doesn't mean
you have to live in a glass house.

INCREASINGLY, A COMPANY'S CASH FLOW
will determine its profit flow.

OVERHEARD OBSERVATION
"He bores me. He likes to talk, too."

HEREAFTER THOUGHT
Many of us better hope that if the Lord deals
out justice, the Devil isn't as bad as he's painted.

WHY IS IT
that the people who always know all
the answers so seldom really have any?

WHY?

Always, all ways, a good question.

WHY DO YOU SUPPOSE

the question from the boss gets more attention than the same question from a subordinate?

SOULS

are not for walking on.

TUESDAY

Toughest day of the week.

It's too far past the good memories of the past weekend, and too far ahead of the next one.

HAVE YOU EVER HEARD OF ANY FREETHINKERS

going to Russia so they can have the freedom to think, write, create, do?

DON'T BELIEVE ANYONE WHO SAYS

British food doesn't deserve its reputation.

BUSINESSMEN IN POLITICS ARE A BUST because, while they see clearly what should be done, they seldom perceive what it's possible to do.

IT'S EASIER TO DO BETTER when there's an audience.

MOST OF WHAT one worries most about doesn't happen.

But who can be sure, if it hadn't been worried about, that it just might have happened?

IF THE PRESS SHOULD EVER BE LOVED it would have to be either lapsed, lousy, or both.

SO OFTEN when someone begins a sentence, "Now, I'm not . . ."—he is.

IN LAS VEGAS the decor of the casinos and the customers are usually a match for each other.

More Definitions

A TAX LOOPHOLE
A deduction that the other guy gets.

ENNUI
An illness, curable by using a Sick Day to do something else.

SOUR GRAPES
turn one's stomach.

ASPIRATION
usually exceeds the requisite perspiration.

EXPERT
I'm inclined to award the title to those whose opinions agree with my own.

GREATNESS
Often hard to detect because it's seldom there.

GIGOLO
A bird of parasite.

POLITICAL REFORMER
One who wants a chance at the trough.

REFORMED REFORMER
One who's having a chance at the trough.

MOGUL GIRTH
Waist of time.

BUSINESS
The name of the game is doing some—profitably.

DEFINITIONS
Uneducated: mental prejudice.
Uncouth: expressed prejudice.
Unpardonable: acting from prejudice.

DEPOSED DESPOT
From shaker to shaking.

HORN-BLOWERS
People audibly conscious of their virtues and who seldom have them.

GOOD INTENTIONS
and good will more often than not *are* enough.

BEAUTY
Outside, it fades; inside, it stays.

IMPOSSIBLE
To eat well and fast rapidly.

PROCREATION
Recreation.

HOME MOVIES
are for taking, not showing.

WHAT'S UNNATURAL SEX?

Having none.

WHAT'S A DIRTY PICTURE?

One that needs cleaning.

COURAGE

is a quality most often displayed
when there's no alternative.

BAD-ISM

Manners help to make life more pleasant.

Mannerisms do the opposite.

NEPOTISM

A very good thing on occasion.
Like if the occasion is you or me.

POWER SEEKERS

Invariably those who are the most powerfully motivated.

TRAVELING

is all the good things said about it
—except for those who constantly have to.

DEFINITION OF PATOIS

French—as spoken by someone else.

SALESMAN

"Salesman" isn't a title. It's a description. Selling isn't something you say you do. It's something you do do, and if you don't, you're not.

SURE THINGS

seldom are.

OLD FOLKS

Those older than thee and me.

EARNING A LIVING

is an unfortunate phrase.
Earning *and* living is better.
The one should never be vis-à-vis the other.

PERPETUAL SIN

Attributing one's own to others.

BEGINNING OF WISDOM

Finding out (after you get it)
that what you wanted isn't.

Father Never Forgot or Forgave Mother

for words she once spoke that shook him to his Scottish core, words that rattled the very foundations of his heritage.

During the spring of booming 1929, she handed Dad a larger-than-life sheaf of bills for the five-children home front, and he exploded: "How in good conscience can you spend so!" To which Mother replied with a happy truthfulness that was gunpowder to my father's fire, "But I love to spend money." From thence to his death twenty-five years later, whenever they differed he'd bring up that remark, considering it the ultimate, consummate condemnation of his wife's mentality.

There's more than a lot of irony, don't you think, that today Mother's philosophy is considered far more essential to our economic well-being than the abhorrence of spending oft expressed by the Founder of *Forbes.*

If he were not already dead, the very thought would have killed him. In fact, it could well be enough to resurrect him.

You Don't Say?

EVERYBODY
has to be somebody
to somebody
to be anybody.

ANYBODY
who tries to be something
to everybody is nobody to anybody.

SOME OF MY BEST THOUGHTS
come with a little good Scotch, while some of my best forgotten ones come with too much of that good thing.

SIGN IN A WESTERN CROSSROADS CAFÉ
"Our pies are dusted daily."

FACT?

Anticipation is most of the fun, but it takes realization of the anticipated to realize it.

THE ENJOYMENT OF LIFE

is most often a matter of mind rather than money—especially if you have enough of both.

MEDICINE'S PURITAN ETHIC

If it tastes good, it can't be.
If it's bitter, it's better.

TOO MUCH TO DRINK

smashes proportionately more writers than drivers.

After one too many, one's "insight" has results that are out of sight.

What makes me so sure? A wee nip of experience.

STUFF OF WHICH DREAMS ARE MADE

isn't dope—except for those who are.

MERRY CHRISTMAS TO ALL
and to all, a not too-cold night.

IF YOU DON'T MATTER TO YOU
it's hard to matter to others.

THE MORE BEAUTIFUL
the hatcheck girl, the less help you
get with your coat. Her job is taking
'em off.

A LITTLE OF A GOOD THING
goes a long way, like garlic.

IF ALL MAIDENS STAYED MAIDENS
there'd be nobody left.

SPEAKING OF DEATH . . .

On the premise that hot air rises, one sure way to rise to the occasion is cremation.
The other way is a sure downer.

SPEAKING OF DOWNERS . . .

The stock market is down so far there's no way for it to go—
but further.

WHAT IS SO RARE AS AN ENGLISH WAITER IN LONDON?

Good spaghetti in Rome.

ONLY THE YOUNG

call attention to the fact that they're older than they were.

SPEAKING OF FOOD

To waste not is waistful.

LIVING WITHOUT LAUGHING

isn't living.

IF YOU LIVE BY THE PRINCIPLES

"eat, drink, and be merry for tomorrow we die," you will.

SQUARING THE CIRCLE
You get more than you give when
you give more than you get.

ACTUARIES TAKE NOTICE
Failing to live causes more deaths
than living to the full.

IN RE-MATING
people tend to repeat themselves

SOME DAYS
are for living.
Others are for getting through.

RUDENESS
An inexcusable form of crudeness.

WRITING ENIGMATICALLY
is often easier than coming to clear conclusions.

IT'S EASIER TO TEAR UP
what you write than to take back what you say.

INTROSPECTIVE

Seventy-five percent of the best I've written (no wise remarks, please) is the result of throwing away 75% of what I've written.

BROWSING IN BOOKSTORES

is invariably stimulating, rewarding—
and expensive.

SATIETY'S

insatiable.

PENS AND MANY PENNERS

write better lubricated.

THERE WAS AN EVENING

The more I drank, the more I thought.
I thought.
That evening.

PROFUNDITY

It's better to be wrong sometimes than all the time.

SAME COIN

Love and hate, psychologists tell us, are two sides of the same coin.

Either emotion makes most humans more so or less so.

A LITTLE RECIPROCITY

goes a long way.

ONE THING LEADS TO ANOTHER

like love and population.

HAPPINESS

is a matter of mind, not matter.

THOSE WHOM CHILDREN

don't delight,
need sympathy for their blight.

THOSE IN THE DRIVER'S SEAT

should be required to know how.

REALITY
What someone thinks is,
is sometimes more real
than what really is.

THE MORE PAINTINGS YOU LOOK AT
the fewer good ones you see.

THERE'S A VAST DIFFERENCE
between painting and being a painter.

REAL JEWELS
don't need 'em.

PEOPLE ARE
the least attractive when they think
they're the most.
Even thee and me.

OBSERVATION
So often, what people are, shows.

WHEN "BEING SEEN" IS THE WHOLE SCENE
it's obscene.

COPPING OUT
is usually better than copping one.

THE ABILITY TO FORGET
is as important as a good memory.
Being able to tell what for which—
ah, that's the key.